Bang Ditto

Also by Amber Tamblyn

Free Stallion: Poems

BANG DITTO

Amber Tamblyn

Manic D Press
San Francisco

The author wishes to thank the publications in which the following poems originally appeared, in slightly different form:

"He Seemed Like A Nice Axe" in *Lamplighter Review*; "Poriferan" and "Face Off" in *New York Quarterly*; "Sunday's Classifieds," "He Seemed Like A Nice Axe" and "In My Best Anne Sexton Accent" in *The Last American Valentine* (Write Bloody Press); "Dear Demographic" (excerpt) in *Cosmopolitan*; "Gene Diamonds" (excerpt) in *MF* and *Spin*; "My Face" (Italian translation) in *Le Voci Della Luna*, *Manifesto*, and *Calla Di Poesia*.

Cover photo: Matt Wignall / Hair and makeup: Alyson Granaderos

Library of Congress Cataloging-in-Publication Data

Tamblyn, Amber.
  Bang Ditto / Amber Tamblyn.
    p. cm.
  ISBN 978-1-933149-34-9 (hardcover : alk. paper)
  1. Television actors and actresses--Poetry. 2. Young adult poetry, American. I. Title.
  PS3620.A66B36 2009
  811'.6--dc22
                         2009024454

for Joan Hyler

Contents

ACHILLES, REVISITED

Arches Up

ROLE RESEARCH

I.

"Jumpers" he calls them, pushing a picture
under my dried tabloid-puke eyes.

The homicide detective at New York's 19th precinct
sits across from me, the mascara maven.

Role research. He has no eyelids left,
just crumpled Polaroids. Murders, suicides,

robberies, kidnapping: seen one 36-year-old
Caucasian male impaled on a pole after

plummeting the length of New Jersey,
seen 'em all.

He shows me his squad's most famous—
an old Pa type, flailing fleshy hoses

chasing a hurricane of illnesses before
shattering his jewel tones into concrete's hide.

Story goes Pa told the cabby to wait
while he went back upstairs to grab something.

He'd forgotten to kill himself so
he jumped right out of skin, planting his broken ass

print into pavement; a grenade's touch.
Forever blowing off that dinner, his mother,

all those knots that took his strings
to Death Row long ago.

In the picture, he's winking at you.
A curved lighting bolt of chompers

dashes across his face, a smile
splashed from impact.

Silly string and party favors
ditching his stomach.

Left index finger doing the vertical jitterbug.
Mr. Potato Head meets Matisse's conception,

or the photo that gets taken while racing down a rollercoaster,
the one you know is coming, so you plan for it.

The detective says it's funny
how he's reminded of the time

he found his son's crayons
melted across a photo of his grandfather.

II.

Gin and Tonic rests between his buttons on Father's Day.
He's nursing someone else's heart, alone in a Cuban restaurant,

occupying a heavy stare at the empty seat across from him.
Ignored by all but his own thoughts that will someday

outthink him. Alone.
I watch, alone.

A waiter tosses him a menu,
a crumb into a coffin.

There are no more quick decisions at his age—
can't have steak without one's teeth,

can't have pasta without a teenager's cholesterol level.
The waiter says he'll come back. Old man wishes for his wife.

She'd know what to do, what to order.
Give him her lemon, take away the bread and butter,

say, "You're too fat, Charlie," kiss his earlobe
on the way to the powder room. She'd pluck

the aches from his brow, toast to all
the old, funny things neither could remember.

I approach his table, bloodshot snow settled in my eyes.
I tell him I'm far away from my own papa.

My heart's been chasing its tail since July 4th, 2006.
I never really knew either of my grandfathers,

except for one of their fists. I shred all
incriminating evidence of confidence.

Bury my hand under my bangs,
eat the last of his olives without asking.

Was his walk home further than mine?
Does he live for her pictures alone?

He looks at the makeup that's carried my face
for so many years, says, "I'm not as lonely as you think I am."

DEAR DEMOGRAPHIC

I'd like to say:
  As a former member of your clique
  (and a current member of your representation)
  I know it's hard to be a young woman ages 18-to 24-years-old.

They put you in a time slot
  that doesn't reflect your views
  with a ratings system
  that doesn't respect your truths.

Listen:
  From one cynical self-hater-by-default to another,
  please put down the magazine article that has bored you
  into hair extensions and reality television.

Stop with the 20th century redux:
  Make your own era. You are not out of your own league.
  Fake eyelashes will not get you Ryan Gosling.
  Nor will sporting a Barack Obama keychain.

No need to break all the rules:
  Just bend them into balloon animals,
  give them to your little brothers and sisters.
  Show them how silly and cute American culture is.
  Time will naturally deflate all of it.

Start mosh-pits in the crowded thoughts of tycoons:
  Stir something up with your tongue.
  Sip someone else's logic then spit it out
  (preferably when they're looking).
  Taste test your own style.

Get your mind into the gutter of others:
  Search for the things they let go down the drain or threw away.
  Everyone's scared to tell you how they really feel.
  Including Oprah.

Stop getting wasted and throwing up
  your individuality outside of clubs.
  There is no fast food to help you cope with that.

Leave your mark on the world
  with something that can't be chosen from
  a tattoo book of Chinese symbols
  for the lower back.

Pierce something other than your skin:
  When I tell you to think for yourself,
  don't give a shit what I say.

BOOK INSCRIPTION FOR 1/2 OF THE COEN BROTHERS

Dear Mr. Ethan Coen:

In the interest of time and saving paper
here's something to read while you're on the crapper—

You're the shit.

Up yours truly,
Amber Tamblyn

FACE OFF

On the bed lays a script
trying to talk my boyfriend
into letting me kiss.

The script, strong and persistent,
tells him that it won't last long.
A six-week affair at most.

It will not spark up
East Coast/West Coast
rivalries of lovers.

It calls for things that make
his body language turn foreign.
Take off my shirt

parade around in front of millions
while he watches helplessly.
The script promises no one gets hurt.

Boyfriend hurts already.
I invited it onto the bed.
Face off.

Boy wants me to do right by my craft.
Do it right without him.
He won't engage a mistress

to the wife of his mind.
After all,
I invited it onto the bed.

But we are both role players,
one art or another,
so what is left to be said?

Tears smell like an ambush.
I know what comes next.

IF YOU'RE GOING THROUGH HELL

If you're going through hell, step on the gas.
Father is always right.

So I grow a heavy right foot,
become a souped-up cock tease with hydraulic thighs.

I don't drive so much as swoop.
Rattlesnake seatbelts and bones for brake pedals.

An eye-mask over the rear view.
A windshield wider than the flesh on a porn star's sternum.

Wipers like the fingers of financiers,
swishing no-no's at the proposals in my eyes.

An overpass reads
WELCOME TO HOLLYWOOD

Guardrails of coke lines lead the road
through the nose holes of Silverlake's youth.

There's an Amber Alert for the missing identity
of a person who has spent her entire life
pretending to be someone else
for a living.

A sign reads
DANGER! ROCKSTAR SLIDE AREA AHEAD

I dodge the falling Hollywood sign letters
and swerve around the road-killed fairytales
of glittering nobodies,

Sideswipe more Oxycontin oxymorons
than a vegan blacking out
in a glass of milk.

A familiar face holds a sign
NEED A RIDE OUT OF THIS LIFE

The next five exits are named
after her worst personal miseries.
Her aura radiates a white chalk outline.

I reach for the radio and bust its front tooth,
let its florescent blood spring sound.
The static stations pitch glimpses
of cold clocks and ketchup hearts to come:

Heath Ledger was found dead this morning. Sources say—

Vote now to guess the date of Britney's death! The winner will receive a free—

Adoption just really humanized children for me, Ryan. As a celebrity I think—

You can get the abs of the stars with Carmen Electra's Aerobic Striptease! Now only—

One million dollars to get Paris Hilton to host your party. She's—

Fake tits are great when your 45, not 14. They make you feel—

Younger is the new black. I'm telling you! If Jennifer Aniston would just—

Die alone. It's my worst fear. To die alone. That, and—

Larry King Live Tonight: Paparazzi...Do they go too far? We'll hear from—

Anna Nicole Smith left behind a baby girl who will grow up to be—

Jane Fonda, Felicity Huffman and Lindsay Lohan star in—

I've, become so numb, I can't feel you there, I'm tired of being—

The #1 comedy in America! In theatres everywhere.

EARTHQUAKE

My entire life has been a huge earthquake
I slept through. All I know are the aftershocks.

The sound of glass being swept up
in my lover's bedroom.

A story I don't remember telling is the headline
of every newspaper the morning after.

My blackouts in big lights.
All I see is the damage I've done.

My mother is the news anchor,
never allowing me to escape her natural disaster.

My father is the kindly neighbor
bringing me a candle and asking about my injuries.

I read a diary full of old
New Year's resolutions:

1) Ignore the commentary on your comical thighs.
2) Write more than just repeating his favorite song's lyrics.

3) Report every shooting star to Mindy while out of town.
4) Tell him you love him before he figures out that you don't.

My friends lie to me like a government.
They say the wreckage isn't as bad as it seems.

My old flames head up relief efforts,
raising money to help the hurt survive me.

My thoughts are homeless dogs running wild.
I just want to know the truth.

I'd like to take the Richter Scale
out for a romantic lie detector test

and when the mood's right,
ask what it really thinks of me.

When it doesn't respond, I'll tell everyone
to sleep in their cars, to move to Florida

where hurricanes announce themselves
before destroying everything.

SEEING INTO SEOUL

His screams ricochet off the hard
helmet of South Korea,
slice through Jung Ju's chin strap,
explode recognition in my ear.

My hearing strains to grasp
a single one of his words
which hang for dear life
from my 13th story motel balcony.

Bricks of a boy's tears
smash the neighborhood,
crack silent shrill instructions
of a shopkeeper to his mutt,

halting marbles where they cascade,
even children
with mud in their eyes
stop slinging looks and listen.

He screams the anthem of a nation
bent over its government's knee,
sold out of a briefcase in the Dai-Moon Ku tunnel,
traded by its mother to a black market,

restless under the bad belly
of its obese Northern brother.
Korea, the mad. An aphid in a cemetery.
A sliver buried in a temple's chest.

His screams turn song,
burning throat's ceiling,
rattling skin and nerves,
flies huddle on my window screen

as it whaps against night's heat.
Mama-sans on the ground below look up,
others just casually walk by.
He is singing the sanity out.

I lunge for the balcony door
tear the fear from his echo's cage
and scream back into pulsating florescent black:
"I HEAR YOU!"

Seemingly, silence. The city
gone to rest after a night of vomit.
Another child caws back, giggling,
runs into a McDonald's.

All that's heard are distant cars
and Big Blue in the sky
leaning over the Namsan mountains,
whispering into depression's ear,

"Congratulations, it's a boy."

ANTE MERIDIEM WITH NOELLE KOCOT
conversation with the poet at Glow Festival

Found, 4 a.m. A buoy advertising
"The Poetry Boat" floats on the festival's map.

She's two miles offshore tasting plum
succulent ancient ring finger dinners,

poems cumming out her drunk.
Once she whispered on a page:

> *I sift through the edges of the wind*
> *and drink to remember you.*

I stumble through sand to find it,
a rotary phone and chair pinned to the beach.

I wait in a line of high school belligerence,
a thousand teenagers opaquely squawking flirtation.

So it seems a thousand. Everything's gleaming here.
Teens have the sweetest of tannins. Their fructose blinds.

But who here really knows the basket of train parts,
Noelle Kocot?

Other poets are on board out there with her,
sharing their desserts with her fork.

Her fork touches her fillings
with the tip of her tongue every 3 seconds.

That's where the poem is first born.
Like virgin births. Trade Winds.

Poppy seed small talk.
I sit down in the sandy chair.

Phone rings. I pick up.
Listen for a deep vocal swarm.

There's a sleeping crowd in the stadium of my ribs.
Stirring. I hear a glass of Fuck clanging in her extremities.

A creaking sublet of a give.
Letting of words. *Hello?*

Hello, she responds.
I'm gonna read you a poem from—

Wait, I interrupt.
Silence.

I'd like to read you something instead, Noelle.
I could recite a poem of your own

or a poem from a book in my bag
by Jeffrey McDaniel called "Absence".

There's a tiny wireless static anticipation.
Moldy lymph-fused rocketships of paralysis await.

She requests McDaniel. She requests
the raking of my lips over her earwax

to create fingers for catching upper case talk.
I read,

"On the scales of desire, your absence weighs more than…"
Any sufficed dull taste of techno-fire,

which plummets from my articulation,
out of this phone cord and into her lap.

She and McDaniel wear long-sleeved loneliness
for the Infinite season.

I am a dribble from a boo-hoo. A tiny,
concentric tingle encircling a cockroach.

"someone else's presence."
Silence.

Wow, she says. *I've always been*
a big fan of Jeffrey's. Thank you.

Goodnight, we say. Hanging up feels like I've made
a matchstick out of myopia's resin but can't quite strike it.

KATHARINE HEPBURN STRAIGHT TO DVD

He's got me by the scruff
like a bad house pig.

The film producer is forcing my head
beneath the water, at the river's equator.

My limbs storming lightning bolt tangos at passing plankton,
hair roping through the water, a drunk octopus at the gallows.

Ten white shovels reaching from my wrist dig into the dirt,
trying to save this little jack-off flesh towel I'm made of.

It's no use—I'm as useless at saving myself
as a zipper in a hairline.

The bubbles trickle up my face;
tattletales sucking up to his hands.

He's hard at work around my neck.
"She's almost out"   *pop, pop, pop*

"Hit her face on that rock"   *hissssss*
Betrayed by my body.

I am an accessory on an Accessory.
All I can think about is

my underskirt exposed up there
where he is, my death provider.

My sockets are burning matches on the asses of my eyes.
My tongue's a rabbit's foot dangling from my face.

My uvula, a sour sardine inverting rot into my cranium,
a poisoned seed sprouting final prayers.

Blood cells take off their hats to water's grand entrance.
Arms: cement covered sockets.

I rise above his hands' stark grip on my skull,
back spasm's finale.

I rise above my self.
There I was, there I am, there I'll be.

My soul's on the bottom of a boot
in Hell's barracks.

A goldfish wedges into the body;
which was mine, now its own.

The fish sings.
"You should have lost the extra 10 pounds."

"Kept your mouth shut."
"Kept your nail polish bright."

"Looked more like someone
who could be looked like."

"Should've never fallen asleep and
dreamt of agreeing to a lakeside picnic

with someone who hates that you eat
more than you do." Stop dreaming.

CROSSING THE WORLD
for Joan

Crossing the world
she buckles under the metal-hooded mouth
of her maker
didn't see it coming

all the women in her

centuries of emotional alchies
daydreaming in distilleries
deep-throating the sallow tongues of sundials
wanting not the backwards
not to fall upon herself like a dagger

she's been under its tires
since the non-beginning
of the women's de-liberation
reversement

been dragged over eras—
Cenozoic speed-bumping her
into the 21st
tugging at her buttons and pearls
digging into the last of her titles

all the women in her

wrapped around exhaust pipes and pit stains
beating her head against pavement
skinning her raw
slow-cooking ribs on rubber rotisserie
tossing out the Tubmans
Woolfs
Di Primas
from her collapsing last impression

its grease
rolling over every feather
all fingers/fading colors
blue eyes
beat black
red thoughts
cocked pink

wouldn't have hit her
        could she be seen
wouldn't have hit her
        had she not been so black
wouldn't have hit her
        had she been he
wouldn't have hit her
        had she not talked back

Oh, if only

she'd let herself be
the vacation spot for prick pit stops
would've pinned her lips
to that politician's dick/a purple heart
for the rash of wrath's backlash

If only!

she stayed by his
Spitzer
Edwards
Schwarzenegger
strayed not
from her Turner!
Run not for president
when no one detonated her
when no one asked her!

Oh, why won't she be

a slant-eyed hut fuck
for a soldier's thrust boar tusk
a Hawaiian delicacy
for the constituencies of Male-Whitey?

Why won't she be
Squaw
Negress
Jap
Turtle
Zipperhead
Yellow-hole
Changa
Puta
or Hilton?

All the women in her
never get rights
only get what's left over
from every hit 'n' run
from every ass pinch to fat fist
from the violent injustices
of our dead sons:

Lennon for singing
"Woman is the Nigger of the World"

Van Gogh for filming
the Koran's hands ripping through
Hirsi Ali's flesh with vengeance

Jesus
for resurrecting
not with the help
of a deadbeat
invisible father
but that of his Mary
and his Mother

the thousands of Iraqimericans
whose commonality consists
of marinating body parts in blood baths

or any young boy
whose throat's gutted by machete
for protecting a single slit
in his family

All the women
out of her
tumbling
thrown to the licensed road lions
to the future drivers of divinity's demolition
garter belt conceptionists
high-heel fuckers

Hollywood hogs
with driveways bigger
than God's complex

crashing us
into lipstick destruction
and false feminine

banging us against
scented stationery
the boss's desk
stapled clits
to the drawing board

Water balloon breasts
busting against humanity's door
under-wire
an ancient snake with a new twist

ripping out our rights to choice
with the wire hangers holding
the sexified dominatrix suit of a Republican "feminist"
the stained cloth commemoration of the 42nd President
the hated dyke-tux of a politician's wife's career flux
after he's caught in bed again with another woman:

Traitors!	Thieves!
Accomplices!	Witnesses!
Aggravators!	Lynchers!
Spies!	Prosecutors!

ALL

crossing the world
bailing from her bodies
hating the mother out of Earth
gifting their guts to the sidewalk serpents
sending ghosts to bed hungry
pulling their pieces to the edges of humanity

curbside delivery of revolutionaries

LEARNING TO TRUST LEGS

Tonight I pumped my breasts with steroid songs.
Strapped six-inch fangs to my feet
and went looking for someone as sharp as me.

Knocked back three glasses of hard easy,
suited up in a hooker's thought process
while toting a 9mm in the cleft of my Kevlar crotch.

It's 6 a.m., a camera's panning across
the yellow tinted bricks I lounge upon
as a cab driver leans out his window

to hail me. "I'm working, you jerk!"
"God bless you," he says.
I'm under 600 covers.

Waddling around 7th and Ave. A
coloring outside of my mind's lines,
collecting off the streets

the things I'll say to Eliot Spitzer
when I meet up with him in jail.
"Go fuck yourself" would be redundant.

Tonight I am criminal,
suction cups and slender death.
I stole the black from a blueberry's asshole.

Go ahead. Ask me why I took the offer
to play a hooker when I knew that you
always loved me more. Ask me.

This Little Pinky

GENE DIAMONDS

Sweating sweet Paris
I sat in Hemingway's writing café
Closerie des Lilas
talked heads or tails with a waiter

whose greasy eyes slid across my breasts,
crashed past the first base of my neck,
unbuttoned my blush with his teeth,
sharking at the smell of my salt.

He wiped away heat from his gums with his tongue.
Asked about my poems and if I would write him one.
I said I no longer commit without commitment.
So he left.

Five minutes later he returned
with a paper napkin rolled up like a ring.
He bent to one knee, soaked in awkward broth.
I accepted the ring, unrolled it, wrote the following:

Dearest Jean Luc—

I don't wear diamonds.
Heirlooms are exempt.
Your Grandma's karma
is your Grandma's problem.

My father stole and gave my mother
a crystal door knob
from a door at the hotel
they could never afford to stay in.

She keeps it on the windowsill,
lets it catch the light and blind her
at random points during the day.
He was in love.

She drank an entire bottle of tequila,
then ate the worm at the bottom.
Told him, "You are rich.
Take a smile to the bank."

It was my father's forearms
that kept her ribs moving,
fingers on the keys
of melodic breathing.

She was in love.
They've been married
twenty-five years.
They're still in love.

So tell me, Romantique,
may I sharpen my teeth on yours?
Don't bring your emotions
into this.

I need a simple
yes or no
that involves little to no
poetics or sweat.

We shall consummate our agreement
between lips covered in fragments of stars
that fell into our hangovers
while we were drunk on elsewhere.

You can write your own alphabet
on the juvenilia of my legs
pressed against your pupils
for the first time.

My thighs are bibles.
Spread the word.
This is not a poem, just a sermon
etched on the bullet I'm placing within you.

I'll burrow into your heart and explode.
Stand at the rubric of what most puzzles you
and bend me brilliant.
Let's find a quiet corner somewhere and beat it up.

Lean onto my mouth,
lower your voice down
into mine like a rescue worker.
Let your chords cripple.

My cunt crunched like tin foil.
Press against my war
with your index and middle
like loaded, explosive double barrels.

Let my trigger pull you.

Amber Rose
of Elsewhere

PORIFERAN
for Shane

There, outlined in your long blue legs,
was the death ray of several shades.
I waited for you to go
so I could watch the colors change.

Didn't visit hospitals
in fear of pastels.
I heard you promised
rain dances in throw-up cans.

Imploded cave-dweller eyes
with coalminer's cough.
The rough in all the diamonds.

On your last day
I brought you my face,
hospitalized by your condition.
Role reversal of the docile.

Suicide bombers threw sweat beads,
you tasted them
wondering what made your
time-bomb lover tick.

At your funeral, you sat behind me
and coughed some more.
Unusually punctual
and still.

I watched from the 10th pew as you
climbed inside everyone's cranial
brown wooden boxes filled with
parts of them that had died with you.

Their parade spread two miles
of impotent, hollow halos.
They smelled the Earth's bad breath
the day it opened to consume what was left of you

in a soft pink rose dress like a tongue
put to rest on the jawbone of death's clench.
Their faces skipped heavy stone tears across
your stone-faced final placement.

"Mom always sounds like she's laughing,"
You hissed from behind me.
"She is," I whispered,
"That's a cry held hostage by regret."

At your funeral, your father
bit down on knuckles
that should have been used
to knock his teeth out.

I remember watching him
try to scale your emotional walls,
built after he confined you
to his kind of prison.

Yes, his maids would be lawyers.
His lawyers would be virgins.
His heart was a mini-bar with
an endless amount of reasons.

I could hear your breath shift
as you shook your head.
Intra-disassociation: you had become
your own crying shame.

I would resurrect your tailbone and serve him
your cop-out stand-offs in meaty proportions.
Your sadness gave clowns the hiccups.
My eyes filled with all your potential.

Our love was small, like airplane bathrooms
and really only good for one thing: relieving ourselves.
So, tell me, are you relieved?
Now that you never get to leave?

THE EVE OF A PRESIDENCY
for Mindy

You get to laugh at
an expense this morning.
Today anything is funny,
at the expense of everything.

There's a permanent cotton candy
glaze over my eyes,
a pound cake of throbbing yeses
at the bottom of my tailbone.

New York buildings are whispering
in each other's fire escapes,
their jaws dropping
ladders to the floor.

Yeah, that's right. I'm wearing
my jeans with no panties on.
They're deep sea diving in the
current of my lover's thread count.

Before the left tit-ache of an election
comes back to taste us once more,
I'm gonna leave his apartment,
walk down Essex St. under beautiful morning sunlight
and leave a trail of life vests behind me.

Let the wind double-dutch in my hair,
turn the heads of every fire hydrant
and pick at my fingernails wondering
how much of him is still under there.

I long for the sigh you make
just before turning off the television.
I miss the way a dance floor
can't find its rhythm in your presence.

The way you hold a glass of red,
the way you say *seriously*.
If your tongue was a postcard, I'd stamp you.
If the crack of your ass was a fault line, I'd 7.2.

Someday, our deaths will make all the tomorrows
stop to look over their shoulders.
Until then, I'm the museum where
your big picture is worth a fortune.

SUBTITLES ON CHILDREN

Walking home from the skate park on Venice Boardwalk with my young niece and nephew, I watch lovers settle into the sand to watch a sunset.

Heads rest on shoulders, making the imperfect outline of a cliff's edge. Some kick sand and salt into each other's mouths and hair, then swarm in to drink the creeping sugars of the night. So many unspoken promises caught in teeth like wisps in the wind.

I remember how my own lover's truancies with my body had grown. We were as likely to last as sand can hold a shape. How he used to tell me my breath felt like the sun setting on the back of his neck.

"Aunt Amber," Dylan says, "why do those people stand there and watch the sun go down? Don't they know it'll be back tomorrow? It's so... LAME."

CROAK
for Bonnie Murray

He sold it out from under his emotional overhead,
where hawks flew in dollar sign formation
above his grief-ridden, earthly duration.

This house built with concert violinist arms,
pine sap and kryptonite nails,
where his wife and three daughters

once grew up summerful and bold as teal's shades,
where their wolf dog, Joshua, nuzzled the sisters
off the dock's end, just so he could jump in and save them.

His youngest daughter, seashell perfect knees,
sifted through the High Sierra's mane
jonesing for Juniper's blood with Bobby Eastwood.

Frankincense would keep the age away,
keep the deterioration of their softball field eyes
and Autumn Aspen pin-curls away.

She was one of
four female walls
that kept him upright.

He sold it, after he and daughters watched
as mother went back to the trees,
back to the cedar vaults of rich soil,

to the thick brandied cloves of death's cocktail.
Cancer had gotten the rise out of her, a black balloon
into the night sky, fallopian tubes like cold wet socks

hung inside her. She was gone
but still stuck to the radiators,
eating through his mind.

He sold it with every ounce of her still inside.
Her final words still floating on the underbelly
of the roof like smoke.

The wolf dog out back, fetching his own bones.
The youngest daughter cried, begged him not to.

He wouldn't hear it. The lake spit against his trousers,
the Aspens coin-flipped silver-green leaves in the sun:
heads he'd break her heart,
tails he'd just slice it wide open.

He broke it like the neck of her guitar
that summer she ran away from home,
a cowboy at her reins.

Broke his family out of it, swung axes
and wrists, ripped the plaster and wires,
broke the croak from which his daughter's sobs swum.

So it's been sold, thirty years or more. A magnificent museum
of the wife mother; All her furniture, wood and iron
organs frozen in past's hell.

The daughter all-grown returns to the kelly green trim,
green to the gills, to look in on the log corpse.
She moves to each window, beating the frogs from her chest.

Every room, time's carnage, a painful proximity.
Carson's Peak hides the sun. Spiders crawl back
into the house's secrets. She longs to fit.

Nothing wants to see her see it,
wants to meet her eyes meeting
her mother's yellow sitting chair,

waiting in the back left corner.
Cloaked in dust. Plates cracked.
The odds she'll ever get the place back,

forever stacked. A widowed dining room table,
its chairs bowed in silence. An unmistakable
fingerprint hiding behind a coat.

A blanket neatly folded over the couch by newer hands
once laid over the last spark of the disease's finale;
a homemade body bag.

Stairs lead down into a quiet cellar memory chamber.
The daughter scans a carpet where she spilt her first years
just as the living room lights turn on,
"Moo is home!!" squeals a child
with seashell perfect knees,
galloping into the living room.

Through the ceiling, the ghost of her mother,
that bunny-eyed face seeps slowly under a bun pulled tight,
sagging into the drapes, slipping down the spatula,

right up to the window, to her 55-year-old daughter
standing before her, staring through the window,
bubbles in their eyes.

The mother fogs the window between them,
her breath softly swaying in the drapes.
Draws a smile with her finger,

which, in a series of moments—
like the house, the one who sold it,
the wolf dog, her ghost, like Bobby Eastwood—

is gone.

FELL OFF
for my father, Russ Tamblyn

I went on your IMDB (Internet Movie Database) page this morning to
remember the film you did with Cecil B. DeMille. The biographer who filled
out your page information, described you as one of the most underrated talents
of our time. Then he wrote about how you seemed to fall off the face of the
Earth for two decades and emerged struggling to find work and so made a slew
of bad films.

"Fell off the face of the Earth," he said, like it's a proud, naturally beautiful
face to begin with. Like the people who couldn't stay under its makeup couldn't
hang on. Maybe it wasn't so much a fall as a tumble. Something all the others
waiting to fall off behind you found funny and charming. You'd hit all of
Earth's collagen and scars on the way down, hanging onto the tip of its chin
and screaming up to Dennis Hopper, "HELP!! THROW ME A HAIR!!"
as Dean Stockwell stood behind him, laughing his ass off. Maybe you did
handstands down the arch of Earth's nose, backsprings across its saccharine
cheeks and glided guideless through the masker's salty, shallow rivers.

Maybe that biographer didn't know
you've never fallen once
off of anything
your entire damn life.

Your hips were born so oiled in instinct
they only had to follow where your mind
had already slid off to.

First base was getting away
from the fame of your body,
nurturing the dark cubes
floating in the collage of tequila glasses
that wallpapered your brain.

Fuck a face you never cared to stay on
in the first place.

On the face of Earth,
you watched as Rogers and Monroe
mummified themselves in its eyelashes,
while Brando and Tracy bent above them,

furrowing at the sight of their theatrical male descendents.
Rock Hudson scrawled his name in lip liner across Earth's mouth,
while Jimmy Dean hung from them like dead skin.

Bobby Driscoll became a blackhead in the cemetery of pores,
alongside other dead, drug-addicted child stars;
memories nobody wanted to touch or clean out.

Elizabeth Taylor had become the big, tacky nose ring
on the face of the Earth.
Balthazar Getty plucked chin hairs with the tweezers of starving artists,
while Natalie Wood forever did the backstroke
in the puddles of Earth's eyes, a moth in a martini.

And all the forgotten entertainers of a decade's youth
made a barricade like a chorus line at Earth's hairline,
doing eternal high kicks in their blue sequins and Tiffany-laced stockings
for five bucks, a pack of Marlboros,
and a chance to even look in your direction.

Your father, the vaudville hustler, is also there.

So you laughed at the face of Earth,
looked out where galaxies were doing things with their lives,
shooting and imploding more dramatically
than any swagger of Joan Crawford's black velvet evening robe.
You saw the paint was peeling above
red-inked fingernails of Jack Hirschman and Michael McClure,
who were writing about the abandoned bowies hung from
George Hermes' patina heart,
in a house built in the curve of Wallace Berman's neck
as he looked up and into you, Telescope;
Both of you, seeing each other from distances,
both of you searching for stars.

He taught you how to close all the books
you never really paid attention to or read,
just so you could open them
and start over again.

You shared stories about the sex, the fortune,
how your father hit you on the back of the head,
teaching you young how to be a bad boy.

Fuck the face you never knew
you never cared to stay on
in the first place.

You fell, you tumbled, you stood with grace.
And even though the Bermans now are disappearing
back into the red rocks, the ants, the golden sand,

even though Glenn Ford could barely remember your name
that day you came to see him crumple his last word
like a bad report card and chuck it at the bed nurse,
you still fell off the face of it all
with irreplaceable style.

So much so that the naked and still nameless
stars on Hollywood Blvd
ripped themselves from the ground
and followed you home
dragging their heavy, lonely edges
that night you learned how to never look back,
to never need the cement
more than it needs you.

RUN ON

I.

Mom brought back El Jimador tequila and cedar from Mexico
I drank some
I peed a lot
never can compute that math
burned the wood
sunk a stone in my kidney
wrote a letter to the devil
punched his face with my language
asked him what's so unlovable about me
he wrote back, said
    love is a liar
    I was adopted
    I was aborted
    after the Renaissance
    before the Holocaust
    close to ghost
    far from Holy
    seriously slacking in the sex department
    yet satisfied.

II.

Why didn't anyone tell me
that vaginas are like small towns
really only good for passing through
in the middle of the night
when no one's looking
while you're barely awake at the wheel
trying to get to the casino
pining to bet all your intimacy
on thirteen black
unafraid to lose it all
walking out in the morning wondering
who didn't take the keys away from you
before you left?

III.

I'm wearing my best Fendi stilettos tonight
Sunset Boulevard is a fine mixture of narcissism and fear
I could mix a cocktail with its breath that could kill your mom
I hope she's not already dead

    That would make this poem awkward
    It doesn't want to be awkward on the first date
    Who does?

you drank Maker's with out me somewhere tonight
which is anywhere I'd rather be than here

Hollyweird
at the valet
waiting twenty minutes for my car
overhearing three girls talk about their pubic cuts
how much their boyfriends like it

    wondering if when he kissed me
    did I taste like wasted time

I'm gonna get in my car and write an epic piece. Call it:
"It's Hard to Face Your Problems When the Problem is Your Face"

    Insert me spitting
    here

I know where petals go when they die.

MY FACE

is a trillion dollar industry, annually.
It carries more advertisement guilt than post-9/11.
My neck is a support beam bigger than Madonna's shoulders.
My tongue's gone into hiding
afraid it might be the next thing to get cut out
like chin fat and carbohydrates.

My spiritual deficit has tripled in size.
Stockbrokers would call it alarming.
God could call it the end of a lunch break.
Indian Nation would call it that bitch, Payback.

I have wrinkles at 22 years old
because they were pointed out to me in the first place.

For an unlimited time only
I can make 'em worse
with a lifetime supply of Diet Coke
and no self esteem.

My happiness comes for free with a mail-in rebate
more expensive than a president's dreams.

I've got skin soothers,
blackhead removers,
night vision goggles
for detecting Charlie in the potholes of my pores.
It's a war zone in my t-zone.
Neutrogena's got the nuke.

My face runs its own nonprofit organization
to help my cheeks raise awareness
and fight laugh lines.

Your favorite tabloid is my philanthropist.
I subscribe to their eating disorder.
Get on my actress's diet.
I'm trying to get back to my birth weight.
I pass it on to other girls so they can learn how to smile
with their rib cages, too,
how to go on a hunger strike in protest
of celebrity anorexia.

Because I am a giver
I share my trillion-dollar market
with the disheartened.
Bond with them
over falling apart.
It keeps us together like estrogen pills and age 60,
like a starlet and a fading star.

I am a giver.

I've got a 1.7 trillion dollar face.
It's worth more than the fight against AIDS.
Been tucked more times than a model's spine
between her legs.
Women's rights look to my face for advice
on how to be uptight.

I am your embassy of Product Placement.

Wear me, little girls.

BARBIE
for my sister

Before we could stutter
each other's existence
or knew we'd have the same
brows and chin

Before we moved into the same 'hood
(your adult and my child)
I kept some form of you
as a Barbie.

I'd act out
sibling moments we never had,
lost by 17 years of our clueless dad,
17 years of your silent mother.

She knew he'd made you, but
knew he'd make you one of us,
so she hid you
up in San Francisco.

I learned the art of imagination
digging for you
in a bottomless, florescent toy chest.
Finding a dolly with your kind of possible pubescence,

I flipped through magazines,
cut out eyes
I thought could be yours
and taped them on.

Barbie had slumber parties
I snuck in on
and got kicked out of
by her older, cooler friends.

I'd cry and burn one of her favorite dresses
in the bathroom sink while she was sleeping.
She had breasts I crushed on,
like I would've yours in secrecy.

I made her the bra
I was never able to steal
from the drawer of your
adolescence.

Was never able
to sling over my tadpole ribs
while you were out becoming
someone.

I wanted to know what you'd think of me,
like a mirror wants to become a drag queen.
Barbie's ass was one
I was ready to grow into.

My sister,
you were an undiscovered eyelash,
plucked up by Jesse Nolan in the 2nd grade,
who squealed "Make a wish! For a Nintendo!"

And even though it took you
17 years to come true,
I still have that sock you forgot
at Dad's house,

the first week we learned how
to make a tiara out of our arms.
To trace our suddenness
in the abyss of each other's absence.

That sock became a sleeping bag
for Barbie, who finally gave me
my own space
on the floor at her slumber parties.

DISAPPEARING ACT

In the morning
your face is clear
as the day it left me.

An iris's dye in the stucco above.
An everlasting thrust of you,
I am a virgin every time.

Broken into.
Your memory is a robbery
where everyone gets hurt

everything gets stolen
and no one gets caught.
May the wind knock you out of me.

In morning, the pillow is a tombstone
where my face is engraved.
My expression epitaph.

Here lies truth.
We lay together in the
unsettled dust of your death.

May sins
forgive you
from your prayers.

In morning,
I am 22 but
you are still 16.

We laugh about it like underage was
an inside joke that turned us inside out
when neither of us were wearing our seatbelts.

You are a car crash
every time, like an accident
when I'm finally prepared.

like the wrong place to pierce a life vest
like the perfect disappearing act
in front of an audience of ghosts.

SOMETHING,
for Carrie

Something
corked your lungs,
taught your stomach fermentation.

Someone
spent your childhood
period.

Somewhere
pedaled bourbon
to your black market blood pump
after your jaw broke young,
eased you into addiction.

Beheaded the piano,
your fingers still in its mouth.

Somehow
took the upper when you started bunking
with barbiturates.

A dictator's liquor cabinet
became more impressive.
It made you rich in Father's liquidity.
His arms, your swing set.
Now just a set of swings
at your face
in memory.

You look crazy ducking punches
while staring in the mirror.

Who beats up who
after death?

Blue eyes go deep,
you always loved the cold love of sharks.

You are statue shards at the air force base,
an arrowhead treasury buried beneath Chuck E. Cheese,
mollusk dust in a stripper's hair,
a hand-woven quilt left in the space station.

THE GOOD HAND
for Brianne

She is a flower child
with a basket of thorns.
Wears white to funerals,
dances the grief out of widows.

No one in Los Angeles knows
how to operate depression
like a carnie show
inside of a casino,
inside of a cathedral

A soft shell with a hard heart.

She goes door to door,
caroling the careful quakes
of shaky immune systems.
Wears skirts to music festivals
so she can pop-a-squat anywhere she pleases.

Never waits in lines.

Thrives on the thought of revivals.
Jumps into religious practice like Dance Dance Revolution.

Has metallic wire eyes crafted
from unwound barbed wires
protruding through the air with cyclonic bloom
pinching hazel from underground harvests.

She'll wonder off and get lost
right in front of you.

Knows exactly what your problem is.

The kind of bravery shaped
by her one good hand.
Her bad hand used to wait
under her pillow for a soft snore,
would wipe away her night sweats
with razorblades hidden in lifelines.

Counted little white meds
jumping over the fence
to fall asleep.

Her bad hand fed her
when her stomach needed a head change.
Drugs left her skin bubbling into wounds
she could not lick with Revlon's tongue.
Left her popping pimples like pills,
and crying out unraveled thoughts
about the lost thread of her dreams.

Genes made her the family hunchback.
Genes made her a harpy of her bloodline.

She had an infestation of remedies:
in drawers, on coffee tables,
under the mattress, (a double-take at floor lint?)
Little edible ants that invaded her walls.

What an unclean house she became,
when the attic filled with chemical cures.

The bad hand liked to threaten the most.
It was constantly feeding bones into her throat.
It painted her pale stems with new skin ribbons,
did all the scratching and cutting,
lifted up layers, looking for silverfish and termites.
Looking for the oppressor.

Even at her lowest, she cut herself
with the same grace that she danced.
Wielding the blade with a plea, lost in music,
in an orchestra of a thousand lovers
that couldn't touch her
but left bruises.

Other women stared at the soul
she bore on a dance floor,
and wondered how to get her style.
She never checked it at the door.

A flower child with a basket of thorns
dances the grief out of widows
wields the blade with a plea—

a caramel in a bowl of pennies.

SHADES
for fathers

I.

Eager and unfamiliar arrived at his front door,
a dawning clasp of his genetic secrecy,
the daughter scraped from his youth's womb.
17-year-old reminder of his off-kilter life,
eyes drunk on Father dreaming,
a second child, born first.

Her breasts carry a plume of mudslide lineage.
He had turned on the faucet, left it running
since the '60s,
there could be hundreds of sapphires
cut from him, he wouldn't know,
couldn't remember,
was too busy balancing the language of Feel
in the center of his handstands
for waitresses on smoke breaks.
Emotional show-off.

The mother never told their daughter.
There was no real respect in them,
those beatnik-nacks she'd twirled in bed sheets with in the '60s
who only extended deep predilection
to Peyote, Indians and Art.

Daughter sweat out the mold of possibilities,
assumed it had to be Charles Manson.
Never trusted a home-cooked meal again.

Sorry, Topanga flower children,
ladies o'The Summer of Love,
The "Sexual Revolution" is on you.
There was love and there wasn't.

Staring at this foreign offspring,
his eyes drooled curiosity.
Somewhere he'd made a sculpture like her,
wings and scapula, balking its wide back.
He wanted to measure her details.
The same nineteen finger steps
from his daughter's navel to her chin

as it was to her mother's, all those years ago.
They must have the same stretch marks
in unusual lighting,
the same clavicle bow to his arrow.
Same solid press of her toes in the night
like a bike peddling to a taste through the fog.

He reached for a curve,
a beacon of his ancient edges,
the kind unquestioned,
statutory sun-screened.
Burn proof.

His fingers went
gracelessly.
Who was he once?

"Dear Father, you are not home.
There is love and there isn't.
I am not home."

II.

A woman came out of the liquor store,
toupee grease on her thighs,
socks stuffed in her pockets.
She spotted him mid-motion,
buckling a seat belt,
wrapping a scarf around his neck.
Probably made by his daughter, that married asshole.

Yes,
his prescriptive bad boy healing routine said,
as she asked for a ride to a motel.
Her eyes weighed oceans.
His hands gripped at 2 and 4.
She wanted the dollar bills poking out of his cock,
his turquoise rings to ping in glossy gut liquid.

Stop here, she said in front of Oceanside Motel.
He signaled pulling over, his blinker a dirty spark plug,
each click a thud from his mid-40s' pillow fights,
the bed frames he'd swung from
like a Chinese star into baby teeth.

As his foot performed flamenco on the brake pedal,
she reached across and touched him.
A past does not promote new dance moves.
No one discovers style by doing the right thing.

Still, his passenger seat swallowed her proposal.
There would be no chemical emancipation,
no rubbers strewn on the hospitality carpet.
No florescent bed-bug after-glow.

The car shook for both of them.

She needed the money or would die
with a million scars unanswered to.
But there were no wolves left in him.
No more questions.

He handed her a hundred bucks,
the green to go
without owing him.

He was growing younger and alone.

She pulled at her pantyhose,
parachutes released,
jumped from the car with Fuck You's in her gums.
Before crossing the street, she turned,
ran back to his driver's side window,
leaned in and ~~hugged him~~
                    ~~held him~~
                    hugged him.

Thank you
            Welcome

LOUISIANA STORIES

I. Johnny P.'s Story
Baton Rouge

"I'm at the Troubadour at a Carole King show, all the waitresses look like Raquel Welch... pissed off bitches. John Lennon and Harry Nilsson came to the bar. Lennon had a Kotex pad taped to his forehead. Nilsson tried to order a drink but the waitress said, "No, you're too drunk." Nilsson pointed at Lennon and said, "Do you know who this IS!?!" The waitress said, "Yeah. Some asshole with a Kotex pad taped to his head."

II. Frenchy the Cook @ Louie's Café
Baton Rouge

"Holy shit! look at all you A-holes sittin' down at my counter.
Now I gotta cook like I like y'all."

"I'll tell you this much... the key to my success has been to fake sincerity. I really mean that."

"I broke an egg in Reno just to watch it fryyyyyyyy!"

" 'DAMN.' That's what a fish say when it hits the wall."

" 'Boudreaux says, "My wife is an angel." ' I say, 'You lucky. Mine's still alive.' "

OVERHEARD: TABLE TWO

My shoes started talking to me, but not the ones on my feet,
the ones in my suitcase. And the damnedest part?!
I couldn't find the key to open it.

TWEET

Look @ all of u. Tweeting twits. Relishing in the whoredom of immediacies. You've evacuated yr brains. Lazy sleuths. I am sad 4 yr pens.

.

Achilles, revisited

TRUST HAIKU

Never trust a man
whose home area code ends
in an odd number.

Never trust actors
who can't cry on cue. Those are
the suspicious ones.

Never trust mirrors.
Image is antagonist.
A recidivist.

Never trust insects.
Especially ticks. Damn spies,
watching me. Waiting.

Never trust trusting
someone who can never trust.
Give it a minute.

Never trust haiku.
Religious, academic,
spiritual. Ew.

Never trust liars.
Unless you yourself are one.
Always trust yourself.

STRANGE

The Death that was coming had come. Between us, always. —*Jack Hirschman*

Los Angeles
>has that Pluto-sized hotel room on Beverly
>and the street with your middle name.
>This is where you first handed me your music in a Walkman,
>flicked off my light-switch eyes
>and we camped out in each other's hair.
>You fogged the letters of a question
>on the back of my neck with your breath.
>Your knuckles rustled through
>waste bins of my waist's skin
>till you found the thing
>that had been ticking.
>Pumping like a trout's mouth
>or the bellybutton of an Olympian.

In Denver,
>my grandmother slipped
>out of the history race
>and I cried you a country
>of the heart's commandments.
>*Jimbo's Lullaby* by Debussy
>guided the customs of our thumbs
>through the borders of our insecurities.
>In twilight, I lit you up.
>We kissed to ensure survival.
>My fingernails scaled the rocks in your back.
>My blue hair fell about your face,
>velvet curtains of the magician's bedroom—
>and into each other's bodies
>we learned how to disappear.

In London,
>we ran the streets
>lost in each other's sleeves,
>laughing at toothless statues
>and stealing hairs from each other's jackets for shrines.
>You screamed up, "I dare you, Cloud!!!"
>as it burst into tears above us.
>We swam into an elevator that sneezed,
>blowing us into our room,
>the smell of the year,
>thick as turpentine

falling from the ceiling.
In the sand of your neck
I buried my head.
Afraid of what was climbing,
my heart pulled herself up the air ropes,
reached the back molars and shouted out,
"I do love you."
It came out as a whisper,
as a tiny thing
you could break like bread.
And into a serious moment,
your lips skipped with me.

In New England,
        at your mother's vacation home,
        I left my silver slip-ons by the sea
        where you wound me like a rotary
        into a back room we dipped,
        out of my slip and into
        my slit you slid,
        the sex had begun to stab,
        bleeding us strange.
        I lay there in your arms,
        an orchid in the trenches.
        Onto her sand we stumbled,
        asphyxiated by gaze.
        You knew how to make the alphabet shy.
        You let it stand on your feet
        and dance with you like a daughter.
        In and out, a tongue,
        a pink teenager,
        you went as a boy
        with an ice cream in August,
        under my black and gray striped dress
        that shed a thousand stories
        around your hips like candle wax.
        We came
        and the ocean wave
        came on us,
        together,
        we fetched the universe
        then threw it back again.
        The afternoon sky shook
        a fat nebulous neck
        crying warnings into our laughter.

New York City
    couldn't take its eyes
    off our getting off.
    On the 52nd floor,
    up against the glass,
    Emptying our dirty dishes
    into each other.
    You counted ribs,
    beat the concerto out of them,
    again and against,
    as the rain too
    pounded us
    52 stories into the blue,
    our skeletons countering
    unspoken stacks of hazardous feelings,
    arbitrary calculations.
    Thunder struck and stuck to glass like ponytails
    hanging on long-legged structures
    standing hard around us.
    A maid walked in on us.
    We were so in love we laughed,
    kept going
    wrapped in a white curtain,
    naked and wet as two Mississippi mummies
    burying each other alive.

Strange,
    how you always
    had some place to be
    some thing to be
    some claim to seize.

Strange.
    In the Catskills
    your eyes grew seismic at the sight of it: me,
    rolling around on the hardwood
    by your black Velcro's,
    knowing you didn't have a kitten anymore
    but a wolf
    in woman's clothing.

Strange.
    In Japan
    your shoulders began to close like hardcovers.
    I could only read your spine,
    faded and dismissive.

Strange.
    Walking around your house in my yellow sun dress,
    that final summer you started shifting the weight,
    smoking like a fish,
    finding the enemy in everything I did.
    Your friends watched me,
    ellipses in their eyes,
    heads bowed to honor
    your next bold move.

Strange
    how you charged me with infidelity
    while in the night your secrets
    spun webs in the corners of your kitchen.
    I could smell her naked
    night swimming in your sweat.
    You always knew how to make
    the best beginnings.

HE SEEMED LIKE A NICE AXE

You were adept in the art of slow recoil.
Not a freckle on your face ever cared to surrender.

I stopped counting the times
I couldn't count on you.

Started the habit of smoking to
forgive your mouth for giving up mine.

Whose lips did you kiss
that last time we did?

You went for them like a draw.
A double dog dare.

You just gazed at the bridge of my nose
while the dams around it broke.

My eyes shrunk to combusting plums,
sadder than a Christmas tree on December 26th.

I should have listened to all the New England fireflies
who told me not to.

My heart was a wave
that broke for you.

BEDTIME FOR THE ARCHIMEDES OF YOUR HELL
poem for my friend whose lover left him for mine

You cried in the grass
to the ends of your aura.
End of an era,
her name subtracted from your teeth's future.

An abyss of stillness
at the speech gates.

Why you ask,
why did she leave you?

She left you
> *because you were leave-able.*
>> *She stopped calling. It seems*
>>> *another had started writing.*
>>>> *She found the hole*
>>>>> *in a different man's heart*
>>>>> *and fell.*
>>>>>> *He was your friend first!*
>>>>>> *You loved her more.*
>>>>>>> *He had a name that publicly counted.*
>>>>>>> *She was great at math.*
>>>>>> *He slipped his hand under*
> *in the dark movie theatre.*

She let him.
> *Let him undress her with eyes*
>> *that your hands used to.*
>>> *His hand used to*
>>> *shake yours casually*
>>> *settling into the secrecy of oncoming casualty.*
>> *The mess of men.*
> *He kissed her.*

You, a silent witness,
a third wheel on their escape car.
> *She left you*
>> *a bandit amongst thieves.*
>>> *Slipping from dark*
>>>> *alleys of their limbs,*
>>>>> *pride wearing a fake moustache,*
>>>>> *crawling between their lips*
>>>> *pretending to be breath.*

Her lies were turning
the blue of your eyes
against the sea.
Even the stars
became constellational conspiracies,
became white polka dots
on the Devil's black dress
as it swerved toward you nightly,
surrounding your dumbfound.
After three years
she left you,
a fraction between
the daylight of her mind.
She might
still or never
remember
a digit
of your smile.

You were a wishbone.
Everything was coming true.

IN MY BEST ANNE SEXTON ACCENT
for the one who shouldn't have

I dug through your shoulders
and found a love poem
you were going to throw away.

I keep it
with all your love letters
in a parrot's cage that dangles from my ear.

I'm a ballerina tiptoeing across your boredom
in a tutu with no underwear on.

My best Anne Sexton accent
sends the caves searching
for their long lost echo
in a sea of yawning mermaids.

Drops by to visit your thoughts unannounced
like the uncle you can never forgive.

Can't keep her eyes off keeping you.

Will wander into the arms of another sense
while grieving for your smell.

Makes the hissing sound of lovers
returning to each other on a holiday.

Doesn't care where your sorrow comes from
as long as it goes somewhere.

Walks the beach at night when the moon is grounded.

Circles the Saturdays in you
hogs all the blankets of your skin

lets you swig on my style
till it creeps up on you like Irish car bombs.

My best Sexton accent
cruises down your post-party boulevard nerves
till something arrests,
is a homeless, hungry journey
into the shelter of your eyes.

Sleeps clutching your sneakers like a stuffed animal
and dreams of running in a world
that ran away with you.

TURNING TO ROPES
for Ian Curtis

Turning to ropes
  his body didn't sway
  the chair didn't look up
  the room only cleared its throat with a creak

Turning to ropes
  his skin bloomed an emerald heirloom soft

A fashionable scarf of a scar would form
  the trendsetting of his throat
  the royal colors of Saturn's rings

A rusty halo that lost its grip and fell
  from the height of his skull
  ten stories of vertebrae to its death
  at the nape of his neck

A bloody horseshoe
  clanging around a tired voice
Footprints of a thousand blue jays
  running finish lines across his Adam's apple

The shape of a noose
  is the shadow of a single petal
  is a balloon crashing back to Earth
  is a boxer's glove defeated
  is the staccato of a tongue
  is a champion's racket
  is a dangling spoon with a reflection
  is one flame curling into itself before going out

Nothing would've made you happier
  than the thought of me finding
  nothing sadder than the thought of
  your guitar   without you

BANG, DITTO

Dear North Star and Venus—

I know you don't give a gas about me.
I couldn't get under your skin
if it was made from damn good tequila
and I was Duraflame.

This life's not retardant.
We'd all love to stop eating
the poisonous parts of our wildness.

The truth is, I feel abandoned
by your thermo-nuclear clubby standoffishness.
I become less your soldier every stray bullet.

You are queens of the sky's Great Revolve.

Nothing revolves around the eggs I've cracked
in the wine cellar, I know.

I couldn't compete with the sun in your fashion,
glistening in its hairline like sweat
from a long, constipated set.
I've heard how those black holes love
taking back compliments.

A woman
is born
every
implosion,
I know.

You've been trying to teach me something.
I can see it in your death's trajectory.
There's less debt in solitude.
Remain without staying.

Those pink scaffolds of yours,
unpredictable and charged,
braise the atomic games of lost marbles.

You are the pair of microscopic floods
getting cried up to nightly,

begging you
to dilute a punch
for an intruder,

tap a shoulder
that bristles with thunder
as fire crawls a staircase.

                    Always recommend rebellion.

Your ever-present bronzed wink
stencils our little nada longitudes.
Chalked up granny's phlegm.

Music has survived off your foreplay.
I know you think this is all funny.

There's no grand equation where I come from.
"Anarchy" is our sad attempt at expressing your footsteps.
Our greatest achievement is the Conscience.
You shit that for breakfast.

Still,
I freehand your big picture
especially when in love.
Extra specially
when out.

Laugh.

FAMILY VALUE

My first son

will be named after my first ex.
He'll never grow up with the Gospel
tattooed to his license plate,
with no cure for a pedigree.
I'll buy him paintbrushes and breakdancing lessons.
At night, I'll dangle a bible from a branch
on the tree outside his window
when the wind is throwing temper tantrums.
In the morning, the curtains will draw the truth.

My second son

will take piano lessons until his fingers weep,
until he's beaten into bravery,
playing Dead Kennedys ballads in every minor key
while counting the lapis above my breast.

The third boy

will be born with bad vision,
will get prescription handcuffs to see through.
He will promise me tragedies,
drop razorblades in my tea,
put dead bees under his pillow for the tooth fairy.
He'll sit in the corner until sorry
for all those times he hit Mommy.

By the fourth one

I'll need a babysitter.
He'll have his father's temper but no father.
I'll catch him nailing his hand to his chest.
He'll say he couldn't remember
where his heart was.
He'll lock himself in the bathroom,
punching his face until his jaw swells
into the man he'd like to become.
He'll ask me to read him my diary
for a bedtime story.
I'll become the woman of his nightmares.

When they all grow up and out,
I'll move to France,
adopt a daughter
and never
give her a name.

FRAMEWORK

You are the mercurial monster of our chemistry.
Ego-slinger. Fiend of blue leathers. King of umbrage.

This journey has become a slither
from a seashell to a cocoon.

Who am I?
You ask me.

I can already taste
the way you'll spit me out.

But my body is a splint,
heart a splinter,

broken off and
stuck inside.

I've got a crutch for a spine,
piggybank spirit.

A desire to murder,
be reborn.

I've got you
to show for it.

I can only prove
that wounds make their own salt

and the sea stole a universe of them
from an unnamed god who stole a parallel one

from the numinous mouths
of lovers like us.

Now go out and find yourself.
Make me want to know you.

HARLEQUIN
for Nancy Spungen

1958 Harlequin
came choking into the world.
Born under Eisenhower foliage,
below the furrow of a distant Soviet,
into the gutters of Philly's liver.

Her cardboard-colored eyes
crested the final pubic inch of her mother
as she threw her first punch
at God
for dangling oxygen above her newborn body;
the first sign that life
was just a decomposable bribe.

An outcast cast out at conception.
A heart thug at deliverance.

Always puking inward,
Nauseating Nancy
did not live.
Temporary survivalist.

Struggle stayed with her.
Twenty years lost in youth comas—
from the playgrounds
beating boys in the face with bananas
to time-out benches
digging her painted black press-ons into her arms.

Spiked collars and rolled up dollars
post psych-ward New York,
she ripped absolutely everything
apart, salvaged only what she could
with safety pins and Percocet.
Her tongue shagged the vowels
of blah blah blah and
fuck you
and while you're at it
fuck punk
and that dick kweef, Rotten.

She belched a contrarian's anthem.
Spoke out against fakers in a faux English accent.

Plunged irony-deep into the satire
of her own knife collection.
Temporary survivalist.

At the Chelsea Hotel,
she swam through her blood on all fours,
the bathroom linoleum riotous with red marble.

A bleach-blond pomegranate
under morphine's anvil.

Dragged her body back to breathless,
how a cat crawls into a garden
to kill a caterpillar before death.

She called out to her famous lover
who was mosh-pitting a harem of heroin
in another room.

1978 Harlequin.
Harlot queen for the Harlem dream.
Manhattan's pink possum.
Nihilist to anarchy.
Hooker lover.

Her loogies still stain the streets of the Lower East,
where she lived out those lyrics she could not sing
and hummed her way into another lifetime,
cooking breakfast for a chair
that moves on its own.

IN A NEW YORK MUGGING

Memories of you
run in gangs all over
this twinkle shit city.
I don't walk alone,
afraid they'll mug me.

Once on Essex Street
one of them crept up behind me
"GIMME ALL YOUR EMOTIONAL PROGRESS!"
I froze.
"OPEN YOUR PURSE AND EMPTY OUT YOUR FEELINGS."

I opened the purse,
emptied out the feelings.
Self-esteem rolled into a gutter,
closure dropped to the cement and shattered.
Slipped guilt into my sleeve,
I always manage to save it.
Grief, insomnia, and depression
cowered in the zipper pocket lining.
They always manage to save themselves.
My recovery efforts,
all of them,
pocketed.

"TAKE OFF THOSE KISSES I GAVE YOU!
WHAT'S IN YOUR POCKET? A PROMISE?
GIMME THAT SHIT, TOO."

I reached in my pockets but
there were no crisp promises,
just a bunch of loose moments and lint.

A punch to the stomach crippled me forward.
"GET ON THE GROUND, FACE DOWN."

I got on the ground,
let it hog-tie me,
my pelvis gnawing at the ground
a soft drill.

My left cheek garnished the Earth,
grated against will.
A cracking kick to the ribs

by a hard, steel-toed break-up
and a consolation friendship
hawked on the back of my head
for good measure.

I lay there,
face in the piss and tears
of all the aftermath in the world,
shoes scuffed from all the years
I tried to climb into his affection
and tap dance.

I stared at the passing ants.
"Please ... help me."

HATE, A LOVE POEM

I've decided to relinquish the rest of the year to heartache.
2006 worked hard and deserves it.

Please think of England when you close your eyes,
because the debt of grief in mine
is about to pay you final notice.

I'm getting you off my chest like dead weight.

I'm getting you out of my system like the lithium
you need to get into yours.

Even if you owe me nothing,
your nothingness owns me.

The last time we slept together felt like it would be.
It was a great birthday present.

Your sex is a broken slot machine that will never change.
It's as intimate as a business card.

Loving you is a casino where sad people spend time
waiting for kings to show up.

Buying into you was a supermarket of regrets.

Heart breaking is a habit you were never broken of.
You're one internet café away from the truth.
You've got more secrets than cells have stems.

I sit in fast food bathrooms, just to remember your smell.
Get cheap manicures to rekindle your touch.
I know your back better than your own shadow.

My fist thinks you're ugly and would tell that to your face.

I'd sleep with your friends.
If you had any.

I'M NOT EVEN ANGRY YET.
JUST SCARED TO TELL YOU HOW I REALLY FEEL.

I'm a death threat tied to a rock
thrown through the window of your opportunities.

In the spectrum of my infinity you are
an all-time black.

Your guilt's so heavy you could tie a noose
and hang your conscience from it.

You led my legs on,
invited my insecurities over for the holidays.

Do your future children a favor
by not having them.

I'd sooner end your life than this poem,
why don't you make me,
I'd like to see you try.
In general.

I'm not jealous of your new lover.
She's just another ring in your dead tree stump.

Now she can enjoy you, Little Yard Sale.
She gets to wear your mother's old clothes.
She gets to rummage around in my hand-me-downs
like I did in the bargain racks before me.

You put the *you*
back in *fuck you*.

MOTH TAMER

Your smile burnt out. Done
with attracting me.

Your laughter, a flame
I'll never return to.

You flick me away with a raspberry slug from your tongue
while stargazing with your new hand holder.

Trap me in your bedroom the night you close all the windows
before making her scream.

I play dead, floating in the glass you sip
before pressing a strand of promises
against her grape-filled lips.

Your porch light yawns,
"Turn me off so she'll go away."

Inside, I chew through her additions
to your sweater drawer.

Land in her salad and take a piss.

Disguise myself as a fancy decoration
on the cap of her perfume.

Take a decade to walk across
her side of our bed
and whisper the lyrics
of an Annie Lennox song
in your ear.

I straddle the tip of your nose
when you snore
and hatefuck it.

Curl up in your grandfather's ring
on the bedside table
and moan.

Die behind the blinds,
antennae touching that thumbprint
smudged against glass.

WITH LOTS OF SALT WATER AND IMAGINATION

We built a dream structure
out of sand and sentiment and called us
the right castle at the right time.

I helped dig balconies and towers
for the shining armor in you.
A place where your dragons could sleep
when you were tired of fighting them.

I carved an homage to your courage
in the form of a drawbridge
so your isolation periods
would always have a form of leverage.

Gave you my buckets and shovels,
the broken glass of a past
worth punching seagulls out of the way for.

We laughed unconditionally,
turned tossed candy wrappers into thrones,
kissed above sand crabs cussing at our nestling kneecaps,
ignored low tides and spirits.

Your face began sinking to the shells,
foundation predicated on disasters,
stung senseless as a jellyfish.

My brain was a bottle
floating away with a message inside.

I should have kept my hands to myself.

INTERLUDE

Are you in love
with that woman
because your songs
must still abide
the peeling seasons
of your death?

You're not the first man
I've flirted with clocks for.

FACE ME

There may never be a chance like it again
to feel the humps on my hips
and their drawbacks, and draw-ins.
The drawstrings
are the curves of my eyes.
Remember how you tugged them when I was shy?

I'm not asking for eternity in the
lunchboxes of future children, but
yeah, face me—

No more imagining.
I deserve to watch your lips stumble.

I want you to remember
every oval on this body,
every tremble into their glory.

Face me, so that I may know the man
who sticks me with goodnight kisses
like a shadowless blade,

like all the silences
in which we were made.

My mouth is an exam
you cannot afford to fail.

Take me.

ODE TO A RUG

Sixteen bloodstains,
one from each bar fight
that followed him back to our home.

A few burn marks and dried green paint.
I used to hide letters under its right corner.
He used to keep the good luck penny
given by his mother before her death
under the left one.

Mousey the cat would take to its center
tracing the sunlight there with a claw,
then get bored, go outside,
ask birds on the telephone wire for a cigarette.

A back burn from an overly excited lover
who sucked on the side of my neck
like it held a *Big Lebowski* sequel.

A collage made with pictures of my grandmother,
an Edie Brickell tape cover
and some poems I never had the guts to print.
I gave it to someone who deserved
so, so much less.

Took my pillow and slept there
when nightmares came down from the ceiling
on a delicate silver string.

Every answered door.
Good-byes.

Sundays spent away from churches.
The last steps of his bulky, clumsy feet.

My hands rolling it up —
placed beside the big blue dumpster
the day I moved into a house
with hardwood floors.

ROADKILL

You deserve to be alone. Okay.
You're miserable. I believe you now,
should've listened the first time you spit it.

Your spine is a road under constant construction.
Your heart lies half-dead on the side of it,
bleeding, barely breathing, and begging for the Lord.

So it took me a few years to hear.
You deserve to waste away like gray.
Okay. You're miserable, I believe you.

You don't need my conviction to feel guilty.
I accept your triumph of comfort and fear.
Stop yelling in a way that only fathers can hear.

I hear you, loud and clear.

You've earned your tire and attenuate, I know.
To sleep in sheets like a ghost without a home
on a mattress that needs braces to match your crooked bones.

House of haunted heart,
may the bottle that drowns out my voice
one day be the coffin you crawl in

to the ground's mouth. Let death
spread beyond the chasm of your obliqueness,
where the fantasy you exude ceases,

the day a non-prophet organization teaches
your prospect lover not to buy into false advertisement.
Forget sweet nothings.

You whispered, "Nothing's sweet,"
long enough in my ear.
I hear you, loud and clear.

SWAGGER HEADFIRST INTO YOUR CAMPFIRE

My only fling has no name.
No one close to me
ever got close to him,
ever saw the ink stars shooting up his arms,
disappearing behind clothes.

My only fling drove the big black truck
I wanted to teach to be reckless
when I was 16 years old.

He was 10 years older but
I was 10 years older
than myself,
so I let him take me
to see a jazz singer
whose name escapes with his,
though I recall a five-minute piano solo
that knocked on my face
with a bouquet of roses
like an old fashioned gentleman.

My fling ordered chocolate-covered cherries,
did as little as rub my knuckle at the table
while we watched the firemen
put out a blaze of strings and keys.

He wore a blue plaid scarf and ivy cap,
far from the scarred eyes and torn hoodies
of Reseda rats that still rested
at the bottom of my brain's backwash vinegar.

My fling brought me back to my car
and I drove off
through his front door
and into his living room
where he played Mingus on 45s
and introduced the handshake of a slow burn.

I lay on his chest and listened to the sound
of an ancient city crumble to its knees.

His heavy belt buckle
stared at my dress

half tucked up over my hips,
a Rembrandt hanging
from a clavicle he could never have.

He kissed, a hummingbird to citrus.
I kicked, a filly in a field.

My fling will never have an ending
to write about. I don't remember
whether I ever called him
my 'darling' again,
or whether he blinked like that
to dream for both of us.

To fall in love
then wake from me.
To know or not know
my real name.

THE BLACK TIE WARREN
for Derrick Brown

Before Mesopotamia was a kiss
shared between two connective tissues,
God or something like it
performed the first ever magic trick
by reaching into a black hole in space
and pulling out two feisty, red-eyed rabbits.

The rabbits terrorized the universe's neighborhood,
putting rocks in the exhaust pipes of comets,
playing horseshoes on their tails,
and whispering to the Little Dipper
what the bigger one really thought of it.

Once the rabbits got the moon so drunk
a drop from its absinthe night sweats
crashed down to Earth,
landing at Hollywood's highly flammable fingertips.

The Black Tie Warren
was where all mischievous creatures
went to connect their dots.

At its gates, a male and female stood.
She wore a dress blue as a gas flame that
clenched her torso like a lover's thumbs.
Her spirit slouched, shrugged like a gut
without a sandwich or a truth.
A copper flower rotted from her ear
and hair slipped down the drain of her cleavage.
Unwashed apples in her eyes.

He wore a dress coat and 1930s civilian boots.
His lullabies couldn't keep secrets.
His heart forgot the lyrics to its own song.
His lungs slept in separate rooms.
His strength grew slender as a cotton thread on a Q-Tip.

Their glass bodies tapped against the doors of the Warren,
pushing through to an Empress seated in a small reading room.
She looked down at the man's sneakers.

"We have a strict dress code. Black tie only.
But since it's almost All Saints Day, I can let you in if
you're wearing a costume. Are you?"

The man placed one hand over his eye, "I'm a pirate."

The woman quickly put her finger to her crimson red lipstick
and painted a stripe from his lip to his chin.
"No. He's a vampire."

The Empress smiled, offering them the entrance door.

Behind them the stone owl on the bookshelf ruffled,
ears swiveled like baby satellite dishes.
The large wall yawned,
rolled its heavy shoulders,
rumbled open.
They stepped beyond
shedding their bodies like sleepy seasons
sliding down a yellow plastic tube
grabbing onto each other's ligaments screaming,
"WE'RE GONNA DIE!"

Their marshmallow bags of muscles
dumped out into the pruned soft bodies
of two young children.

Now a girl, now a boy,
their whiskey breath turned to apple cider,
high heels into roller skates
and neck tie into a puppy's tongue.

The little boy looked up at the portraits
of Thurston, Blackstone, and Keller.
Keller winked.
The boy's eyelids shuffled and spread.

"Look!" shrieked the little girl
"Here come the Lords of the Unholy Trio!
Lord Zabrecky, Lord Fareweather
and that drummer guy from The Pixies!!"

The trio juggled cream-filled jokes,
chucking them in each other's face.
The children fled from the mess to a giant staircase,
steps so big the boy leaned over the edge yelling,
    "GRAB MY TIE!" to the girl, and hoisted her up

into a gold-rimmed hallway,
crooked as a black widow's legs.
The children danced the rhythm
of electric lightbulb candles
while overhead
gargoyles gargled and spit
glittering dust like war cannons.

Each footprint captured by the carpet
belonged to a different animal.
A deer,
a dog,
a lizard,
a crow.

They followed sounds of marching spooks,
waltzing their heavy tire iron laughter through a distant ballroom.

In an olive velvet lit corner,
a sleight-of-hand spider performed
"Now you see eight legs, now you don't!"
to a small crowd of elderly daffodils,
ripping petals from their stamens
and flinging them like Roman call girls.

Out into black water they walked,
onto a plank carved from a shark's tooth.
They jumped.

They floated past a ventriloquist mime,
his puppet speaking in sign language.

Past a huddle of monarch butterflies
in football helmets, smoking cigars.

Past a sobbing ballerina, blowing her nose
into the clothes of a helpless mummy.

Past a row of books on Soaring, Wizardry, and Tectonics
shoved between the heavy, candle-waxed skulls
of Darwin and Sexton.

A 23-year-old Jennifer Connolly
emerged from a crowded dance floor
dressed and dancing a montage moment from *Labyrinth*.
The little girl cooed,
reached out and whispered,

"I will be you when I grow up."

The boy spotted a door cracked open
by a passed-out monkey in drag,
with a bottle of deer's milk stuck in its clutch purse.
The boy leaned down and whispered,
"I will not be you, ever."

They yelped with laughter as an overhead gnome pronounced,
"Behold! I shall be held!"
and high-dived from a blade of grass
into a garden of roses, thumb-wrestling with their thorns.

They ducked from an incoming brigade of sky-diving mustaches
        that quickly unhooked themselves from their parachutes
and ran to make out with the first porcelain dolls they could find.

Disheveled and burnt
glazed and dozing
they stepped into a glass-bottom gondola,
lay down side by side
and watched a frog stuck to the bottom
catch the moss between its gums.

"That's kind of like us," said the little boy.
"You're moldy, and I'm gonna turn back into a prince
once this weird night is over."

The little girl smiled and kneed him in the seed sacra.
When he stifled a cry, she gave him her rusted ear flower and said,
"Suck it up, vampire."

Out of the darkness,
the boy and the girl floated
into the eyelashes of what looked like Planet Earth,
but could've been the cornea of a giant rabbit,
or an 'O' from the lips of the Empress
wishing them Good Night.

ICE CUBE LANGUAGE AND DRACULA BOY

"I have to pound the ring with my fish for this. Oh, you would be proud!"

— *Tamblyn drunk proverb*

INT. AMBER'S BRAIN—LAST NIGHT.

(V.O.) I'm gonna get drunk tonight at this Lucha Libre show in Barcelona. Why the hell not? I feel frisky. What's a bad-ass substitute for Maker's Mark though? Why the fascist fuck can't Spain deliver in the whiskey department?!? Hmmm. What shall be the death of me this evening? J.D. is an obvious and tired choice. I'd never forgive myself if I celebutanted out all over the pool table tonight because I let cheap whiskey tea bag my class. But maybe that's just the kind of self-crucifying an actress NEEDS.

Amber to bartender: "Three Jack's, one Coke please."

Bartender to Amber: "Ha! You are very small-like, for this types of drinkings, no?"

Amber to bartender: "Oh, wait, is this the advice bar? I thought you were selling drinks. I'm sorry, I was looking for SILENCE and HASTE with my order, not a dad."

Bartender: "Ha! Feisty! Okay! I will serve you."

Dissolve into montage sequence

I down three Jack Daniels and wander through the crowd with my friend, Jessica (she's pussying out with vodka tonics). Some strange, handsome type is following me. He keeps dropping directly into my pathway like a stinking Dracula. I'd like to drive one of the spikes of my slut-clogs right through his heart. I smile, coy. Pretend my tight jeans don't hear him.

Jessica and I get tacos at an indoor food stand. She's talking about some obscure musical mash-up reference. I'm counting the melted ice cubes in my stomach. Must be close to 30.

The show begins. Smoke fills the tiny stadium room. A ref comes out on stage: bald and leather-faced like a grandpa's penile skin. *Why is he wearing a waiter's outfit?* the cubes in my stomach ask.

He starts dancing. TAP dancing. Some kind of Flamingo breakdance. Headspins! Booty claps! Pretty sure some colorguard moves were in there, too. He's all over the place. Jessica and I love his moves like a dick in the dark.

Dancers come out on stage to join him… Lakers Girls? Reformed hookers? I question the bulge in the lead dancer's shiny spandex underwear. And, by *question*, I mean *know*. Jessica and I agree, indeed, the lead dancer is, in fact, rockin' a wang thong.

I decide another drink will Unbreak My Heart. (We heart you, Toni!!)

The wrestling match begins. Their Go-Go Power Rangers masks negate the girth of their muscular form. *"Yeah, I got a scary, mean, foaming mouth on top of these flesh nukes, but can you deal with the rainbow of TRUTH covering my face?!?"* Fans in the crowd are screaming as the first round begins. Ripping their shirts off and howling at the dirty fighting. The room smells like hot chorizo breath and salted rims. I feel like I'm at a public execution. My tail starts wagging. The cubes in my stomach tell me I have a tail tonight. I have a real, fluffy fox tail and I'm not afraid to use it.

I order my 75th ice cube and enter my Golden Years of debauchery. Jessica is starting to slur her words. Noticing this, I take a moment to self reflect. ME, TOO.

During the next few rounds, Jessica and I go backstage to take photos with some of the wrestlers. As one of the wrestlers put his arms around Jessica and me for a picture, I slurred something about how much I loved his dramatic, large beard. "That beard is really awesome. It's kinda giving me a baby tent."

"Thank you," his armpit replied.

Jess and I wondered over to the t-shirt table to buy some Lucha Libre tube tops. I asked if they had any shmiddal sizes left, to which the woman said, "Huh?"

Outfitted in our new Spanish feminist tokens, we headed back towards the crowd at the stage. My new Lucha Libre collectors' edition watch read, PIXAR ANIMATION O'CLOCK, which might be something Disney executives scream on a Sunday when they check the box office reports for their opening weekend, but it is definitely a figment of my intoxication. "Rave on, little Libre hands! Rave on!!"

The bell rings as the final round begins. From the chains of mediocrity, hell broke loose. Six wrestlers on stage at once. Really beating the cheese out of each other. Wounds, even. Lucha bloody lipbre—Rolling out of the ring, grabbing a chair out of the audience and breaking it over someone's face. Fans jumping up in the ring like wild beasts. Fans getting bludgeoned, pulverized, and thrown out of the ring like wild beasts. A bra flies through the chaos. A bullet flies through the bra. Someone thought it was a dove of peace. Killed the fucker dead in mid-air. No peace here but pieces. Bells sounding. Murder ballads abound. A tornado of objects and hands and spit. I thought I saw someone throw a baby from the balcony. It was a midget.

Sounds of broken glass and farts. Che Guevara's creaking grave as he rolls over in it. I actually hope someone won't get out alive from this.

EXT. CLUB—NIGHT

The fight spills out in to the street, but now it's with booze, kazoos, masks, and Winston cigarettes. Dracula-boy appears again, right in my sight-line. He stares. I politely smile. Which really means I attempt a wink that looks like I have glue in my eye, and pitch him my signature middle finger.

"Excuse me," he asks, "When was the last time you were kissed?"

Damn. Did he have to bring this up right now? Did he really want to take a ride on my mood swing? I think I ask him to define a kiss. I think he says something about lips that aren't just shaking hands. My eyes dodge the question but my mouth cannot wait to tell him how long it has been ignored. To tell him my lips are like the last empty lot in a world of tract housing.

"What curse is this? May I break it for you?"

Of course, he uses the word "curse." Of course. Dracula boy.

I tell him I'm saving the historic moment for someone else but thanks. *Psyche.* I turn around, run back, and down a whole glass of him. He tastes like horchata candy. He kisses like a slug on Death Row. Someone's calling for me but it's in a language I don't speak at this moment. English is not my current native tongue. So say the cubes.

Fade to black...

DEAR WATERMELON SEED

Thanks for coming to hang out in my stomach last night.
You are so clever,
the way you snuck into my mouth like that.
So clever, aren't you!
One of the reasons I fell for you, to boot.
I could have sworn your friend Watermelon
was gonna want you to stay but
I'm glad you came over anyway,
despite how it ended between us.

You are so small and round in person,
much darker than you look in the pictures.
Much more of a "fun guy" than the tabloids
at Whole Foods have you chalked up to be.
Might I add—
a chip off the old farming block.

Seed, I want you to know that
pooping you out wasn't intentional
nor malicious. Please don't cry little juice tears,
or get lost in the crevice of some woman's teeth,
or drown yourself in the disgrace of a mixed fruit bowl.
Don't let your life go down the drain.
Please don't cry the fertility out of you.
I never meant for hurt, this I swear.

There were rumors that you were trying to "harvest" a child
in my small intestine, which led to
my colon's hasty (and might I add, a tad rude) removal
of your little body cavity from within me.
Colon is an old bird, more jaded than an Indian headdress—
this was to be expected.

Though you are long gone,
I will always remember you.
If I left your heart with bad feelings
I hope you don't harbor them there,
just dock them for repair.

The memories are ultimately where it's at.
Like the time you got lodged in my tonsils and
tongue spent two days trying to pull you out.
(I still laugh about it to this day).

The time I burped after that ginger ale drinking competition,
and you popped right back up in my mouth yelling, "Tally ho!"
Damn near gave me a heart attack.
The time I ate those "bad blood" cousins, the cashews?
You told me you needed space.
I gave you a rocket ship and a match.

The time I found out that a man hated me
just a little less than he hated himself,
my heart went out and crushed herself.
Shriveled up into a prune
like a deflated, ripped balloon.
You sunk down there right next to her
and held her for hours
while she cried the kind of red stuff
that reminded veins why they are blue behind closed pores.

Little prune heart found solace in you.
Chewed up and spit out, you knew fruit very well.
I hope you have found a nice mound somewhere.
Perhaps even a cow pile.
(I heard those help you grow twice as fast,
especially the ones way out in California.)

I hope you fall in love with a beautiful watering can.
I hope your children are as delicious and healthy
as you are.

Tell them about me.
About the good times.

About how I spilled my guts
and shared my insides
with the only thing
that ever dared to grow with me.

Your soilmate,
Rose

SUNDAY PAPER CLASSIFIEDS
for Pablo

Cloud Seeking Cloud
For Rainbow Genocide

Must be able to speak four species of bird
including pigeon, seagull, and hawk.

No stratonimbus mood swingers please.
Shape-shifting as a hobby is a plus.

NO BUTTERMILK GOD COMPLEXES
—shifting into someone's dead cat
to make them cry is not original.

I enjoy creating phallic restorations,
        tornado teasing farmers,
            and stealing spotlights from all things blue.

Willing to trade skills:
        Airplane rattling (a good laugh when someone pukes)
        for the art of sunset making. (I can never get those rays right.)

 Must be lonelier than I am.
Are you with me?

If so, meet me above Mount Everest tonight.
I'll be floating next to the big, glowing white magnet
on God's black fridge.

WINTER

He is that illustration drawn in pencil
where once there was a window.
Now color.

A shape so unrehearsed,
he is sprouting unknown shades
referring to themselves
in the third person.
Monochromes wait for him to dry.
New color.

A paint truck spilled in summer.
I want to roll in his thunder, dry off
by walking backwards against the rain.

Leave my chest blushing
early plucked, in season,
out of ripe.
I am the between-cartwheels-and-summersaults
of his out-of-breath childhood memories.
Catch me.

Between the U and the S,
sky falls,
we slip into symphonic blues
like honey woven hula-hoops.

His tongue stirs water in my hole, hollow.
I blow kiss bubbles through
to meet his cracked windpipes.
Mouth to mouth fizz fights.

May I always decorate him
without seasonal reasoning.

I see life as a glass half-full squared,
but only when he's in it.
Bring two straws.

AT THE NATURAL HISTORY MUSEUM

Dear Mammoth—

Please come back
and share this cake with me,
as I know how much you love frost
and I hate frosting.

Plus I want to ride your tusks to the boardwalk
and make all the palm readers cry.

WORD WAR

Love came home an unknown.
Came home to me a mystery.
Went to its death

withered as dried spit.
The lamb of lions returned
on crutches disguised as legs.

Love returned from the war of
relationships, adulteries and affairs
with secrets it never shared.

People wanted to hear it all firsthand—
How many casualties? What kind of weapons?
Did Love get to see the bodies?

Love stayed silent. Spoke only
of knife holsters and leafless trees.
Counted hairs on a bar of soap.

Charged them with treason.
Soaked in the pool for 12 hours,
staring up at the red mountain ridge

then went looking for a palm reader.
Declared hearts as but empty shells from its shotgun.
Took dinner plates to the bathroom.

Flushed any unnecessary leftover liquids.
Sometimes the spoon. Made jokes that
blowing out its mind would really blow mine.

Love came home an unknown.
Crawled in bed like a crippled ape,
stayed there staring down thin air.

Mug compacted to a dent.
Breath an abandoned cave wind.
Once, while sleeping,

Love awoke,
caught its fist staring at its face
in the dark like a wolf.

Love screamed out,
a prisoner in a palace of nightmares,
an orphan to an apron.

Love hid under the house
in a cellar built from scrap paper,
each piece scribbled with illegible definitions on self.

Love was a commie noun,
a languid lie of universal language.
(One of *Them*.)

Love studied itself until its teeth ground out,
mad and sick to indifference.
Found them on the floor later,

pointed and screamed in horror
"LICE!" Looked us in the eyes.
"I'm dying of lice, you murderous species!"

Love threw the teeth into the fish tank
hoping to drown the bastards,
but one of them, a molar,

knocked Sally The Fighter dead.
Love stared, shocked.
Wept against the glass,

a five-year-old meeting Christ's image
crucified for the very first time.
Love went to apologize, couldn't speak,

reached into the tank, grabbed little white rocks,
jammed them up into the blood of volcanic gums
like little dead sailors stuck in pink mud.

With the other hand,
Love grabbed the dead fish,
kissed it, a mouth full of crimson crayon.

Words formed into snakes from the gaps of sanity.
"Don't ever forgive me, Sally."
Love came home an unknown.

Slowly died before us.
It was not within us to know why.
Helpless ourselves,

bedridden rudimentarily
from mystery.
Had we done this?

Had we made Love sneak trysts
with arm hairs and needles?
Made Love reduce itself to

a plastic deer crumpled over in the front yard?
Love looked at us with 20/20 hindsight.
Went to its death snagged

by the hopefuls of the Hail Mary.
Went to death with a world of
other's cards and letters.

Mental tar and feathers.
Went to death with secondhand
symbols of self.

Went to death
pennies short of thoughts,
poor and swollen.

Watched wood crosses
in window frames turn holy.
Love we didn't.

Lover and I
we did not.
We could only apologize for being straws.

We could not ease the pain
of vanishing numbers of lovers like us,
destroyed over the years.

First kisses. Blushing of tongues.
We all assign each other forgetting.
The bathing of throats.

We didn't believe in Love enough to let it change us.
No human changed from Love.
We grow smaller each day without.

Another break up,
another rose on Love's grave.
It's not within lovers to know why.

The insects and I swarmed
a white sheet over Love's body,
Goodbye.

SCHOOL FOR THE VIVID
for Beau Sia

You were going to tell me we both
had the same dream last night. I know.

We already spoke of it, remember? This afternoon,
during the nap I usually take before dream class?

That tiny, vivid rummage.
Tonight, I'll study it.

Your face resting in my lap
like a severed tulip's head

drooling into the beginning snow.
Remember?

Make a promise. Bury it
in your tongue till Spring.

DOWNER'S CLUB

Down
there she falls asleep facing the window.
A bright index of gravity's concubines.
Aphid by sheer proximity.

Down
there her guts are sisters she has disowned.
Blunt barbs of flesh; cannibal feminists.

Down
there she dreams of a job that exists
at the bottom of an ocean.
It dims to blue apartment fire color.
Bricks glow from the mutiny of algae.
Cold salt fog rolls against misplaced bones,
its dandruff confuses sand.

So much
        misplaced.

Up
here her ears ring
in the constant cumming of a city
that heaves above plexus.

Up
here there are more blisters than scabs,
more stairs than hallways,
more shades than exposures.

Up
here she does not know
the night's sky from the inside of a mouth
that might've swallowed her whole.

A phantom in a drain.
A tunnel which has no dawn.

So much
        remains.

IF YOU DECIDE IT'S BETTER TO LET GO
for Joan

Let go.
I'll cherish the sorceries of your past
with every ounce of my couth.
I'll decapitate the headaches in your fire.
Collect your intention's protégés.
I'll take good care of them.

I'll put your pearls in small suitcases.
Send them back to the beginning
of your neck, when sunlight first kissed it.
Back to the beginning
of Pacific's hunger for your balance.

Let go. I'll hang on
to the husks of your tender song.
The stray volts untamed
by magnetism's mantra.
Summer salads and fresh salmon,
in your honor.

I'll keep the memories
of night-blooming jasmine
pickled on your breath,
of the sea's salt filling your room
like petals from a lover.
The sounds of ocean waves,
applauding your feet every time
they touch a balcony.
That which crashes
into, not against you.

Let go. I'll give back
your fingertips to the pulse
of any intimate conversation.
To the first waterfall
that throbbed between your breasts,
as they slid down and found the source.
Back to my back,
how you loved to hold
the better part of my beast.

The loss of your skin
will not sweep the spells of
your handwriting away.

Let go.
I'll send your physical ruins
off to the pollen gods.
Ta-ta, molecular dungeon.
Your beauty in strength,
the history of a galaxy
inspires bumble-bees
to grow silverbacks.
Your battered legs are
the bats of Ty Cobb.

Let go.
We'll toast to your spine,
our limbs lamenting nothing;
You are life's eternal drip,
the algorithm that answers to no one,
the punk years of chamber music.

And you won't be missed.
You cannot be missed
if you forever exist.

OH, YOU
for David

Look at the way your dirty socks stare
at all my dirty underwear.
Our love beats the love
Hemingway had for Paris,
the kind marriage carries for swans. As long as
homosexual swans are included in marriage.
Otherwise, no.

You are my bandana soaked in holy water.
This is what I call whiskey,
when I'm tying your sweat to my forehead.

When I'm closing in
on your multiple noses
like a sorority party kiss.

We're not drunk always.
Just forever.

That's our book title,
our mantra, et cetera
our quenched life's climax.

I bargained with the world's
greatest dicks for you.
Not talking statuesque.
Just pricks. Ask any diary.

You are the most confident Tijuana.
You are Sheriff's powder and the secret
to why pretzels taste so good.

I want to be the bullet that crashes the party
of all the women who ever tore through you.

You are a barcode of drum rolls across my thigh on a subway.
You are a scribbler of figure-eights on the trunk of my hips.

Your initials have replaced my teeth.
You are everything that smiles about me.

And lastly—

You have the most beautiful, tiny, tight ass.
I reach for it more than I complain that Frente
never put out a second album.

At night when I crawl into your bed,
wasted as a trash heap of pearls on the street,
listening to you sing Nickelodeon songs while showering,
my left breast leans over to my right one
and high-fives it.

COLD CONSCIENCE

The Big Freeze has been pedaling cognac
to the serotonin mafia that runs these bitter streets;
we are all walking heartbeats looking for something to eat.

The colder it becomes, the more hardy our screams.
The herb cabinets are breaking loose.
Pierogi and bigos under down comforters,
ham hocks and black-eyed peas under the heat lamps of our eyes.

There are alley marches in the Villages,
everything Fall is on sale:
trees are giving out free leaves,
vintage leather blue boots and hot cider.

There's a soulmate on every corner
with a cigarette and a need for someone's fire.

Bums meet in Thompson Square Park at noon for a memorial;
Tiny Sad Tommy got a job in the L.E.S.
C'est la vie, booze comrade.

Henry the Hawk came back to his branch
after two years on the West Side.

Our chests are chimneys, our lungs al dente.
The sewer's steam, a street remedy for achy feet.

The Chinese water beetle who was there,
in the corner of my kitchen window—
the specimen I'm supposed to report to Health and Safety—
is gone.

We were all here, once.

I've gathered the collective conscience of Avenues A through D.
Pricked every phone conversation to California with it.
Begun to miss the way Los Angeles never goes out of season.

My lover and I sleep in till 2,
eat eggs at 3,
find a way to light something by 5.

A case of broken wine glasses lie in the street.
A couple argue through mouth-covered scarves,
tongues particularly tied.

Everything sex and supper.
Everything super and sax.

Post womb-marinate, I tortured my mother's nipples in my infancy. Grabbing onto one with my gums, I'd stare her down, stretch it way out and release, snapping it like a rubber band back into place. My baby laugh was more menacing than the sound of a villain jacking off to a thunderstorm.

When I was seven, I cut off the entire bottom of my parent's friend's curtains to make a dress for my Red Sonya doll. They were sleeping and Red Sonya had appointed me Queen. The doll wanted a train and a train she would get. I found nothing wrong with it. Part of me still doesn't.

At eleven, my parents went on a trip to Africa and left me with my neighbor's mom. They also left her their car to drive around while they were gone. No one ran this by me, so I decided to take the car away from her. I got into the Chrysler while all the kids from the neighborhood gathered around my chaos like birdfeed, staring on with big O's in their mouths as I searched for the emergency brake release. I coaxed one of them, Fallon, to get in and ride shotgun so she would know what it felt like to be a part of history. I drove the car around ¾ of a block before smashing into a parked car, right in front of a neighborhood mom, Susan. She didn't flinch: Amber was at the wheel of a car and Fallon was in the passenger seat, eyes barely over the dashboard and shaking? Sounded right.

At fifteen, I decided to test out the most infamous Worst Nightmare. I walked onto my high school campus completely naked, a blue Jansport backpack over my shoulder and Pumas on my feet, with six pubes to my name. I got as far as the first quad of the school before getting tackled with a coat by Mr. Rupprecht. Of course, to complete this experiment, I would've needed to let the boy I had a crush on *see* me naked. But that never happened, nor did I have a crush on anyone who went to my high school. I wasn't so much sheltered by my life as a teenage actress as I was exposed to those who needed to condemn me for it. I learned quickly the importance of experimentation and secrecy.

At sixteen, I got my nipples pierced the same week I won a *Hollywood Reporter* award for my role on a soap opera. The following year, I got a tattoo on my shin of what my mother used to call "The Bad Fairy" when I was a child. Also known as the Karma Fairy, this mystical creature would force me to ram my hip into a coffee table after talking trash about the girl next door's glass animal collection. (My mom liked to anthropomorphize aspects of Buddhism and Native Americanism. She still calls herself a woman of "Christian values.") As I would scream in pain, Mom would scorn, "What'd you say mean about somebody? The Bad Fairy gotcha!"

When Mom first saw the tattoo—this great Tinkerbellian monster she had created—she announced, "Amber Rose, I'm gonna take that off with a cheese grater!!!!" To this day, I wait for the Bad Fairy to give her hers.

I guess it's fitting that after losing a movie role to the blue-eyed, whoopee-cushion-tits screwing the Executive Producer with his finger on the green light, I slipped into the ugliest mood I could find, bought a bar of 80% cacao, let a swig of whiskey pray at the altar of my ribs, and went out to pick a fight with the first religious center I could find. I found myself entering the shack where actors get fixed: the Scientology Center of Toronto.

Ingesting chocolate chunks and hiding behind raccoon black shades, I saw a man approaching me. He asked what he could do for me.

"I want to buy *Dianetics*," I told him, thinking about what my boyfriend would say later over the phone. ("…WHAT!?!?!?!")

"Alright. I'm Jim. Why don't you 'step into my office'? " he said, swishing quotation marks with his fingers. He found this very funny. I couldn't stop thinking about the girl with whoopee cushion tits.

Jim took me over to his "office" which was an open desk next to several others, like a car dealership. On the desk, a picture of Jim and John Travolta holding each other longed for me to be as happy as they were. I thought, *What's so wrong with being a little lost with people who have found their loss and truly embraced it?*

Jim asked that I first listen to a few things he had to say about their center before buying the book. Whatever, I had all the time in the world. He launched into a speech about feelings. Do I have them? Am I in touch with them? What is sadness a direct descendant of? In the family tree of despair, which feeling has been lynched most throughout the centuries? What is 4 + 4? Was I sure?

I nodded. I laughed. I held a fart. I had moments of silence. After the oral presentation, Jim asked if he could put me in their mailing list system, just as someone in an office chair rolled into my periphery, leaning back and asking, "…Hey, aren't you that girl from *Sisterhood of the Traveling Pants*? Amber Tamberland?"

I began to sweat. Shoved three more pieces of chocolate into my mouth. Wasn't this what Scientologists were famous for? Figuring out your identity then, without further ado, having you killed? I told her I was not but had often been mistaken for "Amber Tamberland."

I told Jim I didn't want to be put in the system. He then asked if there was a credit card I'd like to use for the books.

"Ha!" I laughed. "Cash only, Mr. Card-Carrying Member of People who Need to Carry Cards." Jim, the girl in the chair and I all laughed, threatened as endangered species.

I took my *Dianetics* purchases and walked back home. The sounds of the day died around me and as I shot them full of dirty looks, I opened my front door to find my dad sitting on the couch. His gray hair puffed out over his head like a Colorado thundercloud, the way it had always done after his naps. His eyes looked like ancient soaked maps in mud puddles. His big soft cheeks took flight around a semi-toothless smile. He offered me a Maker's Mark as my friend Jessica came down from upstairs to join us. I showed them the *Dianetics* test booklet and told them the story of Jim.

"Did I ever tell you girls I used to use the "Scientology Chart to Nirvana" as a dart board?" he asked us. "I only pegged the center 'CLEAR' once, and that was when I was on mushrooms. Go figure."

Dad read from the *Dianetics* test booklet, leaning forward with his elbows on his knees and adjusting his glasses. He began to write down the answers to its questions:

Question #1: *Do you agree that man needs a science of mind?*
Dad: "I believe he needs a silence of mind. These are not simple questions."

Jessica and I nodded. *Word.*

Question #2: *How is the* Dianetics *term "recall" arrived at?*
Dad: "TRICK QUESTION!!"

I took off my sunglasses to lessen the glass between us.

Question #3: *What are imagination and creative imagination?*
Dad: "There's no difference. Who wants to smoke a joint?"

What's the difference between aberrated and unaberrated perception?
    "You should go stick your head in a toilet," Jessica said.
    "EAT SHIT," I quickly added.
    "Oooooo, that's good!" Dad said, writing them down.

Okay, next question! *Describe "Returning."*
    "The truth is right in front of you, when your back is turned."
    "Something to do with Blockbuster Video."
    "Going in a circle. Duh."
    "Editor's note: to avoid this, use condoms."

What are the attributes of Clear?
    "Makeup looks nicer."
    "You can see the fishies at the bottom!"

Describe what you believe an Optimal Individual would be.
    "I don't believe."
    "Can we pick ourselves?"

Give another example you have thought up of a Held-Down Seven.
    "Question 11 was way better."
    "Is that a poker term?"

Acknowledgments

Thank you to the people who have been closest and most nurturing to me in the heavy four-year process of creating this book:

My papa Russ, Jack Hirschman, Bucky Sinister, Rob Sturma, Jessica Townsend, Buddy Wakefield, DEDLY Eddie, Keeli Shaw, Brianne Gates, Megadith, Ross and Heidi, April Jones, America Ferrera, Alexis Bledel, Harris Hartman, Gideon Yago, Stephen Latty, Kristin Taylor, Mercy Audiss, Tiffany Huff, Shawnee Penkacik and everyone at Amtam.com, Rebelasylum.com and Manic D Press; my marathon poetry partner, Derrick Brown, who is a better friend then a looker; Bob Holman and everyone at the Bowery Poetry Club; Beau Sia, for the numerous ways in which you are a caretaker; and Jeffrey McDaniel, for the friendship and the extra pair of eyes.

Special thanks to the following women who are and have been the very guts that I follow: My mama Bonnie, Alla Plotkin, Jillian Fowkes, Cari Ross, Bonnie Bernstein, Michelle Bohan, Leanne Coronel, Jennifer Joseph, Tilda Swinton, Mindy Nettifee.

And that one chick, David Cross. Of course.

About the Author

Amber Tamblyn has been a writer and actress since the age of 9. She has been nominated for Emmy, Golden Globe, and Independent Spirit Awards for her work in television and film. In 2007, she won the Locarno Film Festival Award for Best Actress in the film, *Stephanie Daley*.

Amber's writing has been published in *New York Quarterly*, the *San Francisco Chronicle*, *Teen Vogue*, *Cosmopolitan*, and *Interview*, among other publications. Her first book, *Free Stallion* (Simon & Schuster) won a Borders Books Choice Award for Breakout Writing.

She is the executive producer of "The Drums Inside Your Chest," an annual poetry performance event in Los Angeles (thedrumsinsideyourchest.com). She is co-founder of the non-profit organization, Write Now Poetry Society, which works to identify, inspire, record, and publish great poets and strengthen poetry organizations (writenowpoets.org). She currently lives in New York City.